THIS BOOK BELONGS TO:

_____

_____

P IS FOR PILGRIM

P is for PILGRIM

THE CHRISTIAN FAITH – A JOURNEY FROM A to Z

Stephen Cottrell

Illustrated by Jack Seymour

First published in Great Britain in 2024 by Hodder & Stoughton
An Hachette UK company

1

Copyright © Stephen Cottrell 2024
Illustrations Copyright © Jack Seymour 2024

The right of Stephen Cottrell to be identified as the Author of the Work has been
asserted by him in accordance with the Copyright, Designs and Patents Act 1988.

The right of Jack Seymour to be identified as the Illustrator of the Work has been
asserted by him in accordance with the Copyright, Designs and Patents Act 1988.

Unless stated, Scripture quotations from *The Holy Bible, New International
Version*® Copyright ©1973, 1978, 1984, 2011 by Biblica, Inc.®
Used by permission. All rights reserved worldwide.
Scripture quotations marked KJV are taken from *The Authorized
(King James) Version*. Rights in the *Authorized Version* in the United Kingdom
are vested in the Crown. Reproduced by permission of the Crown's
patentee, Cambridge University Press.

A CIP catalogue record for this title is available from the British Library

Hardback ISBN 978 1 399 80527 8
eBook ISBN 978 1 399 80528 5

Page design by Isobel Gillan isobel@isobelgillan.co.uk

Printed and bound in China by RRD Asia Printing

Hodder & Stoughton policy is to use papers that are natural, renewable and
recyclable products and made from wood grown in sustainable forests. The logging
and manufacturing processes are expected to conform to the environmental
regulations of the country of origin.

Hodder & Stoughton Ltd
Carmelite House
50 Victoria Embankment

To my grandchildren

SC 2024

INTRODUCTION

FOR ALL OF US, LIFE IS A JOURNEY. If you're reading this book, the chances are you've already come across Jesus. You may not know much about him, or the people who follow him or the faith, Christianity, which bears his name.

As you explore this faith, whatever your age, you will soon encounter some challenging words: Trinity, Sacrament, Reconciliation, Sin, Incarnation; even the word 'Christ' itself. It isn't Jesus's surname! It is a title with a meaning and history.

SOMETIMES it might feel easier to avoid these difficult words.

SOMETIMES it might feel fun to enjoy keeping it difficult, as if faith was like some hard exam you couldn't ever pass.

SOMETIMES it might feel easier to settle for a dumbed-down explanation by using other terms instead.

SOMETIMES it just feels embarrassing to ask. So, are 'Eucharist' and 'Communion' the same thing? Everyone at church seems to know. Or at least *act* as if they know.

Sooner, or later, these words, and the ideas behind them, must be addressed and understood. It is simply not possible to be a Christian without understanding sin and forgiveness, without knowing what a sacrament is, or without accepting Jesus as the Christ.

This book is here to help. It explores and explains most of the key concepts and ideas that underpin the Christian faith.

I had assumed that someone else had already written a book like this. It seemed such an obvious thing to do. But while I could find weighty tomes on the topics explored here, I couldn't find a book which covered all these things in ways that were accessible, comprehensive and friendly: a simple book about complex things; one which just about anyone could read and find helpful.

So, I wrote one.

My name is Stephen Cottrell. I am the ninety-eighth
Archbishop of York, and since I believe that teaching is
an important part of what a bishop is supposed to do, *P is
for Pilgrim* aims to be a resource for Christians of all ages,
providing an introduction to the basic words, ideas and concepts
that you will encounter as you journey in faith and become part
of the Church.

I wasn't brought up going to church, and this is a book
that I'm sure would have helped me when I first explored
Christianity.

P is for Pilgrim belongs in every Christian home. It's a
book for schools and Sunday schools. A book for Baptism and
Confirmations. A book for parents and children. A book for
a newly confirmed teenager to keep by the bed. A book that
a godparent can look though with their godchild. A book for
parents to have in their bag when they accompany their children
to church.

But it is not simply a children's book. It is for adults as well,
providing a set of reference points for anyone who wants to
understand the Christian faith.

This is a beautifully illustrated book. and the pictures tell an important story too.

Therefore, read the pictures as well as the text, as you enter into the profound beauty of the Christian story. Ask yourself, 'Why *this* picture on *this* page? What do the pictures tell us that the words can't?'

P is for Pilgrim explores the deep mysteries of some beautiful but complicated words, but I know that all our words and all our explanations fall short of the beautiful and mind-blowing truth which is God and how God is made known to us in Jesus Christ.

Finally, in writing this book, I have tried to be as faithful as I can to the inherited traditions of the Christian faith that the words convey, but I can't help but write from the perspective of my own experience of living as a follower of Jesus Christ. Therefore, the book, its words and its pictures, tell a story: that coming to faith is a journey; the whole of life a pilgrimage home to God and to the banquet of heaven; that Jesus shows us how to live well, and that around God's table there are places set for everyone. These are the ideas that have particularly shaped my faith.

If you are searching for meaning in life and want to know more about the Christian faith, then this book is for you.

You can read it cover to cover. Or dip into it now and then.

It is about growing in faith, and it is about God's great desire in Jesus to count everyone in.

It is an A to Z. Or as Jesus said of himself, a beginning and an end.

A is for ADVENT

The word 'advent' means 'coming'. Advent is about an arrival – the arrival of Jesus.

The Christian faith begins and ends with Jesus, the one God sends into the world to show us the way. Jesus is God sharing our life.

Advent Sunday is the first Sunday of the Christian year. The four weeks of the Advent season prepare us to celebrate the arrival of Jesus at Christmas – and at the end of time, when Jesus will come again.

'For the grace of God has appeared,

bringing salvation to all.'

TITUS 2:11

A is for Adventure – the great adventure of the Christian faith.

A is for Alleluia – the great Christian shout of praise.

A is for Apostle – the first people Jesus called to follow him and the first people he sent out to share his message.

A is for Amen – which means 'I agree'.

A is also for Adam

The Bible begins with the story of God creating the world and declaring it good. Then comes the story of Adam and Eve, the first human beings. But they struggle to be good. Like the rest of us, they do things that they know are wrong. Right at the beginning we discover that left to our own devices we human beings tend to muck things up. We need help.

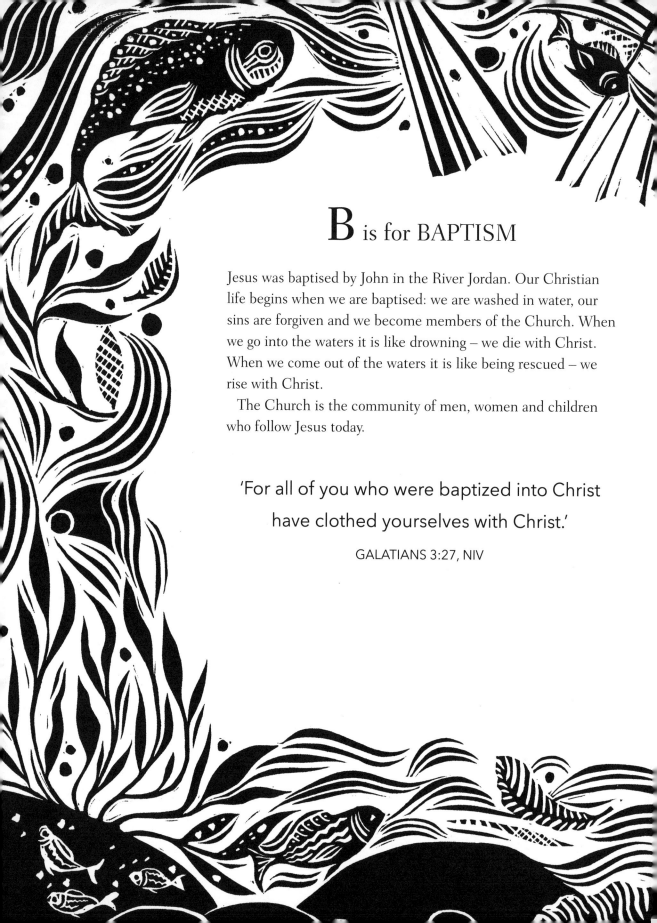

B is for BAPTISM

Jesus was baptised by John in the River Jordan. Our Christian life begins when we are baptised: we are washed in water, our sins are forgiven and we become members of the Church. When we go into the waters it is like drowning – we die with Christ. When we come out of the waters it is like being rescued – we rise with Christ.

The Church is the community of men, women and children who follow Jesus today.

'For all of you who were baptized into Christ have clothed yourselves with Christ.'

GALATIANS 3:27, NIV

B is for Beginning – the new
beginning of the Christian faith.

B is for Bishop – those called by
God to serve and lead the Church.

B is also for Bible

The Bible tells the whole story of God's love and God's purposes
for the world.

The Bible comes in two parts. The Old Testament (also called
the Hebrew Scriptures) tells the story of how God made the
world and how that creation got spoiled; then how God chose a
people whose job it was to show the world the way. But they also
got it wrong.

The New Testament tells us about Jesus. God sends Jesus
to show us how we are supposed to live and what life with
God is like.

C is for CROSS

The central event of the Christian story is the death and resurrection of Jesus. Jesus shares our life on earth so that we can share God's life in heaven. On the cross Jesus even shares our dying. God raises Jesus to life on the third day to show that we have a future with God. The cross is our pathway back to God. The resurrection is our first taste of the heaven God has prepared for us.

'For if we have been united with him in a death like his, we will certainly be united with him in a resurrection like his.'

ROMANS 6:5 NIV

C is for Christian – those who are marked with the sign of the cross when they are baptised.

C is for Church – the body of believers in Jesus.

C is for Christ, which means 'God's anointed one'.

C is for Christmas. The child born in the manger grows up to be the man who dies upon the cross.

C is for Creation. We are meant to care for it!

C is also for Confirmation

At confirmation you declare the Christian faith for yourself. The bishop lays hands on you and prays that God the Holy Spirit will bless you and guide you in your Christian life. You are literally 'confirming' your faith and promising to follow in the way of Jesus.

D is for DOVE

The Bible says that when Jesus was baptised, the Holy Spirit
came upon him like a dove. When we are baptised and
confirmed we receive the gift of the Holy Spirit. The Holy Spirit
is the invisible power and presence of God that is available
today to help us to be like Jesus.

'Then [Jesus] said to them all, "If any want to become my followers, let them deny themselves and take up their cross daily and follow me."'

LUKE 9:23

D is for Diversity – God made a beautiful, diverse world. The Church is made up of all people from all nations. The Holy Spirit speaks all languages. No one is outside the love of God. We need each other.

D is also for Disciple

The word 'disciple' means 'follower' or 'learner'. It is what the first friends of Jesus were called. We are Jesus' disciples today. We follow him and try to live like him. We learn from him about how to make the world a better place and how to live as God intended.

E is for EVERYONE

The Christian faith is for everyone! In the Bible it says that when you become a Christian you are united with Jesus as part of a new humanity. In this humanity, barriers are broken down. Gender, sexuality, age, race, class, colour – none of them prevent us from knowing God. None of them separate us from God. God has created the world and the human race in wonderful diversity. All are welcome.

'So in Christ Jesus you are all children of God through faith.'

GALATIANS 3:26 NIV

E is for Easter – the greatest celebration of the Christian year, when we remember God raising Jesus from the dead.

E is also for Evangelism

After the resurrection, Jesus ascends to God. He tells his disciples to share his message of hopeful love with all the world. Evangelism means telling people – everyone! – the story of what God has done in Jesus. And what he's doing in us today.

F is for FORGIVENESS

There is a cost to Christian faith. Jesus begins his ministry by telling people to repent. 'Repent' means 'turn around'. It means living differently. It begins when we say we are sorry for where we have gone wrong. It means facing up to the fact that we have said and done things wrong and that the world is not as it is meant to be. The Church has a word for this. It is sin. And there will be consequences we have to live with. But the Church also has a message. It is forgiveness. With Jesus, we can be forgiven. We can start again.

'As far as the east is from the west, so far he removes our transgressions from us.'

PSALM 103:12

F is also for Faith

Jesus shows us what living differently is like.
Faith means having faith in Jesus as the hope
for the world and the hope for our lives, forgiving us
and bringing us back to God. All this reaches its climax
when Jesus dies on the cross. God shares our life and death
completely. Then when Jesus is raised from the dead, we
see the final sign of God's power over sin and death, and the
promise of life with God for ever. This is our faith.

G is for GOSPEL

The word 'gospel' means 'good news'. The good news is that
nothing bad – sin or death or evil – will ever have the last word.
It means that whenever things feel desperate, or whenever
you feel lost, there is hope. The good news is that God is with
us in Jesus and continues to help us through the power of the
Holy Spirit.

'For God so loved the world that he gave his only Son, so that everyone who believes in him may not perish but may have eternal life.'

JOHN 3:16

G is for Gift. All this is free. It is not something we can earn. God loves us and wants what is best for us. God gives himself to us freely in Jesus.

G is also for Grace

Grace is the merciful, loving presence of God reaching out to us, especially when things seem desperate and when we are feeling lost or hopeless. One of the most famous of all Christian hymns begins with the words 'Amazing grace'.

H is for HOLY COMMUNION

On the night before he died, Jesus had supper with his friends. At the table, he broke bread and said, 'This is my body, given for you.' He took wine and said, 'This is my blood, shed for you and for the forgiveness of sins. Do this to remember me.'

Ever since then, Christians have gathered to break bread and share wine in remembrance of Jesus. This meal (which is also called the Eucharist, which means 'thanksgiving') helps us understand what Jesus' death on the cross means – his body broken, his blood shed. It is also the way in which Jesus is with us today.

Eating the bread and drinking from the cup is the main act of Christian worship. When we do this, Jesus feeds us with his risen life. The bread and the wine become for us the body and blood of Jesus. He is with us now as he was with his disciples then.

'The cup of blessing that we bless, is it not a sharing in the blood of Christ? The bread that we break, is it not a sharing in the body of Christ?'

1 CORINTHIANS 10:16

H is also for Heaven and for Hope

For Christians heaven is not just the place we go to when we die. It is something that begins here on earth when we follow Jesus. Receiving Holy Communion is one of the ways we share in the life of heaven.

In the Old Testament, Moses and the people of Israel were fed with manna from heaven. Holy Communion is a bit like our manna from heaven, until that day when we shall see Jesus face to face and share in the banquet of heaven. We call this the Christian hope.

I is for INCARNATION

Incarnation means 'becoming flesh'. It explains the first great truth of the Christian faith that, in Jesus, God became a human being like us. As it says in John's Gospel, 'And the Word was made flesh, and dwelt among us' (John 1:14, KJV).

I is also for Inclusive

Although Jesus was born as a first-century Palestinian Jewish man, what is really important is that Jesus was human. Therefore, all humanity in all its amazing variety is included in the love of God who shares our humanity in Jesus.

'Let the same mind be in you that was in Christ Jesus,

who, though he was in the form of God,

did not regard equality with God

as something to be exploited,

but emptied himself,

taking the form of a slave,

being born in human likeness.

And being found in human form,

he humbled himself

and became obedient to the point of death –

even death on a cross.

Therefore God also highly exalted him

and gave him the name

that is above every name,

so that at the name of Jesus

every knee should bend,

in heaven and on earth and under the earth,

and every tongue should confess

that Jesus Christ is Lord,

to the glory of God the Father.'

PHILIPPIANS 2:5-11

J is for JESUS

Jesus, the Son of God, is the centre of the Christian faith. There is no Christian faith without him. The word 'Jesus' means 'God saves'. We reach out to him, because he reached out to us.

Jesus told lots of wonderful stories. One of the most famous was about two houses. One was built on sand and the other was built on rock. They both looked the same. But when the storms came, the one on the sand collapsed and the one on the rock stood firm. Jesus is our rock. We must build our lives on him and follow in his way. Then, when the storms come, even when death comes, we will be safe.

'You show me the path of life.

In your presence there is fullness of joy;

in your right hand are pleasures

for evermore.'

PSALM 16:11

J is for Joy. The way of Jesus is the way of true happiness
– that's why there's so much singing in church!

J is also for Justice

Wouldn't it be wonderful if the whole world built itself on Jesus and lived the way he shows us? Then there would be an end to poverty and violence. We would live in a world of justice and peace. Everyone would flourish. The creation itself would be safe and well. Following Jesus means building a world on his good foundations.

K is for KINGDOM

Jesus spoke a lot about God's kingdom. But it isn't a place. The kingdom is where what God wants to be done is done. Therefore, it can be anywhere and everywhere.

Jesus said that it is very precious, like treasure buried in a field, or like yeast making dough rise. He said that it is worth more than anything. He said that it could make an amazing difference. But God's kingdom doesn't really have a king. Or not as we expect. Jesus the Servant is on the throne. And the throne is a cross.

We continue to live in the world, with all its beauty and opportunities, but also with its problems and challenges. We follow Jesus the Servant King. We try to live his way and build God's kingdom on earth as it is in heaven.

'Jesus said, "Let the little children come to me, and do not stop them; for it is to such as these that the kingdom of heaven belongs."'

MATTHEW 19:14

K is also for Kindness

One of the best ways of showing that we are part of God's kingdom is by little acts of daily kindness to our family, our friends and our neighbours. These little things – like yeast in the dough, or like a mustard seed growing – make a big, big difference.

L is for LENT

Lent is the season before Easter. It lasts forty days, reminding us of the forty days and nights that Jesus spent in the wilderness before his ministry began. In Lent, Christians try to sharpen the pencil of their being a disciple of Jesus.

By reading the Bible, saying our prayers, attending church faithfully, saying sorry for what we have done wrong and thinking carefully about how we can be more like Jesus, we grow as disciples. Of course, we must do these things all through the year. But Lent is a time for a reboot.

'[Jesus said,] "I give you a new commandment, that you love one another. Just as I have loved you, you also should love one another."

JOHN 13:34

L is for Last, Least, Little and Lost. Jesus showed special care for those who were on the edge, for little children, for people who were weak or sick, for the vulnerable and for those who found life tough. So should we.

L is also for Love

One of the most famous passages in the Bible says that what
we do isn't really worth much if we don't have love. This is so
important. We could read the Bible every day, say our prayers,
go to Church every Sunday, and appear to be the best Christian
ever, but if we don't love God, love our neighbour and love
ourselves, then it won't make much difference. Jesus gives us a
new commandment: to love one another.

M is for MERCY

You can never be reminded too many times that God's very nature is love, and that because God loves without condition, God is always merciful. Therefore, even when we continue to get things wrong, and especially when we are not very loving, God's mercy is poured out to us. That's why most church services begin with a confession, where we say sorry to God and acknowledge our need of God and ask for God's mercy. It is why we must be merciful to each other. We know how much we need it ourselves!

'He has told you, O mortal, what is good;

and what does the LORD require of you

but to do justice, and to love kindness,

and to walk humbly with your God?'

MICAH 6:8

M is for Mission. God is a missionary God.
He sends Jesus into the world. Jesus sends his disciples.
We too are sent by Jesus to share the good news of God's
merciful love – by our word and our actions.

M is also for Mass

This is another word for Holy Communion or Eucharist. Like
the word 'mission', it comes from the Latin word for 'send'. It
reminds us of our responsibility to share what we receive.

N is for NEW

The word 'new' appears many times in the Bible. The story of Jesus and the first Christians is called the New Testament. The apostle Paul says that when we become a Christian we are a new creation. The psalms tell us to sing a new song to the Lord. Right at the end of the Bible, in the very last book, God says, 'See, I am making all things new' (Revelation 21:5).

New is for new life, new hope and new beginnings. The Christian faith is new every morning.

'The steadfast love of the LORD never ceases,

his mercies never come to an end;

they are new every morning.'

LAMENTATIONS 3:22-23

N is also for Nicene Creed

The word 'creed' means 'belief'. A creed is a summary of what Christians believe about Jesus and about God. The Nicene Creed and the Apostles' Creed are the most famous. They are often read in church services. As we say these words, we declare our Christian faith.

O is for OUR FATHER

When the disciples asked Jesus how to pray, he taught them the prayer that we call the Lord's Prayer. These words of Jesus tell us everything we need to know about prayer. We are taught that God is our Father; that we must praise God and seek God's will and God's kingdom. We are told that we must be sorry for our sins and forgiving to others; that we must ask for what is enough and not for more; and that God will be with us to save us in trial and temptation. It is a prayer we should learn by heart and say every day.

O is also for Ordination

Everyone who follows Jesus has a part to play in God's mission of love to the world. But just as Jesus called twelve apostles to a particular ministry of leadership in his early Church, so he calls people today. Men and women serve the Church as bishops, priests and deacons. This is called ordained ministry. Ordination is the service during which people are anointed by the Holy Spirit for this work.

Our Father, which art in heaven,
hallowed be thy name;
thy kingdom come;
thy will be done,
in earth as it is in heaven.
Give us this day our daily bread.
And forgive us our trespasses,
as we forgive those who trespass
against us.
And lead us not into temptation;
but deliver us from evil.
For thine is the kingdom, the power
and the glory,
for ever and ever.
Amen.

P is for PILGRIM

A pilgrimage is a journey to a holy place. Christians go on pilgrimage to Jerusalem or Canterbury, York or Walsingham, or other holy places associated with Jesus and the saints.

Human life is a journey. It begins when we are born. It ends when we die. When we become a follower of Jesus the journey of life that ends in death becomes a holy pilgrimage that leads to life.

When we follow Jesus and walk his way, we become pilgrims.

'Blessed are those whose strength is in you,

whose hearts are set on pilgrimage.'

PSALM 84:5, NIV

P is also for Pentecost

Pentecost is the feast of the Holy Spirit. The disciples received the gift of the Holy Spirit. They were able to talk in many languages. This enabled them to take the message of Jesus to all the world. God loves variety: not the whole world speaking one language, but the Church speaking every language. Today the Holy Spirit is also enabling us to share the good news of Jesus with everyone.

Q is for QUIET

We have spoken about prayer as saying things to God. The Lord's
Prayer is the pattern for this sort of praying. But sometimes
prayer can be silence. Sometimes prayer can be just sitting
quietly with God. One of the psalms says, 'Be still, and know that
I am God.' Sometimes the best prayer is the quiet that comes
when we simply rest in the presence of someone we love. Who is
the person you love the most and who loves you the most? Being
with God in prayer can be like being with that person.

'Be still, and know that I am God.'

PSALM 46:10

Q is also for Question

Jesus asked his friends lots of questions, like, 'Do you love me?' and 'Who are you looking for?' It made them think.

And they asked him many questions too. To ask questions is good. To ask questions is natural. We must ask questions of God. We must ask questions of each other. It is how our faith grows.

R is for RECONCILIATION

'Reconciliation' means 'to make things right'. And if you have an argument with a friend, someone has to make the first move in order to make up.

The amazing thing about the Christian faith is that although God has done nothing wrong (all the problems are with us!), God makes the first move. He does this in Jesus. It is as if God says to us: you know all those things you've done wrong? Let me take the punishment for you. Then we can forget about them. Because I love you and I want you to have life with me, even the life of heaven.

'Be kind and compassionate to one
another, forgiving each other, just
as in Christ God forgave you.'

EPHESIANS 4:32, NIV

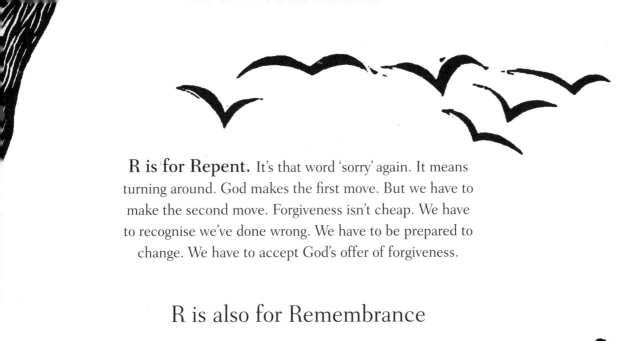

R is for Repent. It's that word 'sorry' again. It means turning around. God makes the first move. But we have to make the second move. Forgiveness isn't cheap. We have to recognise we've done wrong. We have to be prepared to change. We have to accept God's offer of forgiveness.

R is also for Remembrance

This is the word Jesus used at the Last Supper: 'Do this in remembrance of me.' Do this and I will be with you. Remember my love for you.

S is for SACRAMENT

A sacrament is an outward and visible sign of an inward and spiritual grace. What this means is that God uses ordinary things – like water, bread and oil – to do extraordinary things. They become one of the ways we receive God's grace today.

The first two sacraments were given to us by Jesus himself. The others have developed in the life of the Church over the centuries.

> 'They devoted themselves to the
> apostles' teaching and to fellowship, to
> the breaking of bread and to prayer.'
>
> ACTS 2:42, NIV

S is for Sin and Salvation. Sin, as we have discovered, is when we get things wrong. Salvation is God putting it right.

S is also for Saint

A saint is someone who has been put right with God and lived a life of holiness – even if only seen and known by God.

S is for Seven

There are seven sacraments.

1 Baptism

2 Eucharist
(Holy Communion)

3 Confirmation

4 Healing

5 Reconciliation
(sometimes called confession)

6 Marriage

7 Ordination

T is for TRINITY

Jesus is God's Son; God sharing our life on earth. Jesus teaches us to call God 'Father'. When Jesus ascended to God the Father, he sent the Holy Spirit, who is also the presence of God. As the first Christians thought about all this, they concluded that although there was only *one* God, God was known to them in *three* persons – Father, Son and Holy Spirit. We call this the Trinity: God is three and God is one. God is a community of persons, but still the one God.

'May the grace of the Lord Jesus Christ, and
the love of God, and the fellowship
of the Holy Spirit be with you all.'

2 CORINTHIANS 13:14, NIV

T is also for Ten Commandments

These are the laws that were given to Moses in the Old Testament. They form the basic framework of a good, honest life.

U is for UNIVERSAL

In the Nicene Creed we say that we believe in one holy catholic and apostolic Church.

'Those who hope in the Lord
will renew their strength.
They will soar on wings like eagles;
they will run and not grow weary,
they will walk and not be faint.'

ISAIAH 40:31, NIV

The Church is *holy* – we are in community with God.

The Church is *catholic* – it is universal, the worldwide body of believers, the Church in heaven as well as the Church on earth.

The Church is *apostolic* – it is built by Jesus on the foundation of the apostles and, like the apostles, we too are sent out by God to live and share the Christian faith.

U is also for Unless . . .

One of the psalms says, 'Unless the Lord builds the house, the builders labour in vain' (Psalm 127:1, NIV).

This means we need God's blessing and guidance for everything we do. Jesus said that if we are cut off from him we can do nothing. He is the vine, we are the branches (John 15: 5). There are lots of ways of expressing this each day. Little things, like saying grace before meals to thank God for our food. Big things like loving our neighbour and working for a world where everyone has food to eat.

V is for VIRTUE

A virtue is an admirable quality in a person. So virtuous behaviour means excellent behaviour. It means, for instance, following the Ten Commandments. The apostle Paul goes further. He says that the highest gifts are faith, hope and love, and love is the greatest of all. This is more than just keeping commandments. It is displaying an excellence of love in everything we do.

'Brothers and sisters, whatever is true, whatever is noble, whatever is right, whatever is pure, whatever is lovely, whatever is admirable – if anything is excellent or praiseworthy – think about such things.'

PHILIPPIANS 4:8, NIV

V is also for the Virgin Mary

Mary is sometimes called the first Christian. She said yes to God and became the mother of Jesus. She could have said no…

Mary lived out these virtues. She had faith in God. She hoped to see what God was doing in Jesus fulfilled. She showed great love. She stood at the foot of the cross when others had fled. Mary can show us what loving God and believing in Jesus looks like.

W is for WISDOM

Wisdom and knowledge are not the same thing. Knowledge is the things we know. Wisdom is more about how we live.

The Bible is full of wisdom. Jesus told astonishing stories, like the Good Samaritan and the Prodigal Son, which help us to understand how we should live. Whole books in the Bible, such as Proverbs, are about wisdom.

'Do not forsake wisdom, and she will protect you; love her, and she will watch over you.'

PROVERBS 4:6, NIV

W is also for Way

The first Christians were called 'followers of the Way'. We are disciples and pilgrims following in the way of Jesus, learning wisdom and working to build a better world.

X is for . . . KISS

When we send someone a birthday card we put a little cross after our name. The 'x' represents a kiss. It shows we love that person.

God plants his cross in the heart of the world for the same reason: to show us love.

Jesus went to the cross forgiving the soldiers who nailed him there and promising the thief dying alongside him that today he would be in paradise.

In Greek, the word 'Christ' begins with a big X.

The cross is God's kiss to the world. Jesus Christ is the one who delivers it!

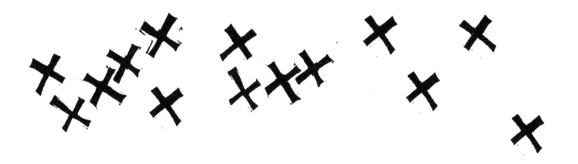

'Greet one another with a kiss of love.
Peace to all of you who are in Christ.'

1 PETER 5:14 NIV

X is also for even more kisses

Because we kiss things we love, one of the best ways of understanding what is happening in the Eucharist is to look out for all the kisses.

As the service begins, sometimes you will see the priest kissing the altar table. Why? Because this is the place where we meet Jesus as we share bread and wine.

As the deacon finishes reading the Gospel, the Bible is kissed. Why? Because we meet Jesus when the Word of God is announced.

When we share the sign of peace, we can kiss each other (or just shake hands)! Why? Because we meet God in each other.

Y is for YOU

You are a child of God. You have been made in the image of God. You are precious in the sight of God.

The Christian faith is for you. If you were the only person who ever lived, God would still have reached out to you in Christ. That's how vast and how deep God's love is for you.

You matter to God. God has a picture in his heart of the person you are meant to be. God wants you to become that person.

And you can become that person – full of faith, hope and love – by living your life with God.

'For the Son of God, Jesus Christ, who was preached among you by us . . . was not "Yes" and "No", but in him it has always been "Yes".'

2 CORINTHIANS 1:19, NIV

Y is for Yes – your yes to God and God's yes to you!

Y is also for Yesterday, today and for ever

In the letter to the Hebrews in the Bible, this is how Jesus is described: 'The same yesterday, today and forever' (Hebrews 13:8).

Z is for ZENITH

The word 'zenith' means the 'highest point in heaven'.

The last book of the Bible is the book of Revelation. It ends with a wonderful vision of a new heaven and a new earth. God makes everything new.

'These are the words of him who is the First and the Last, who died and came to life again.'

REVELATION 2:8, NIV

Z is also for Zed!

Z is the last letter in the alphabet. And that is the end of our A–Z.

In the book of Revelation, Jesus says, 'I am the Alpha and the Omega' (Revelation 22:13). The letters Alpha and Omega are the first and last letters of the Greek alphabet. In other words, Jesus is saying that he is the A–Z. He is the beginning and he is the end.

Jack Seymour is an English teacher, graphic designer and illustrator – he's worked with various organisations including the British and Irish Lions, Land Rover, Google, Ordinance Survey and The Stewards' Trust as well as illustrating books and book covers. He works in lino, etching, monoprint, pen & ink and watercolour.

Author of many books for children and adults, Stephen Cottrell is the Archbishop of York, one of the most senior posts in the Church of England. However, his life's work as a priest as well as a bishop has been to tell the story of the Christian faith in ways that are simple, compelling and lovely. This little book is just one more way of explaining and telling that story.

When he isn't 'bishoping', Stephen loves to walk, cook, eat and write. He also makes lino prints, though not nearly as good as Jack's, though somehow one managed to sneak its way into this book!

Stephen is married to Rebecca, who is a potter. They have three sons, two grandchildren and one dog, Molly.

I am hugely grateful to everyone at Hodder for their support for this project: the beautiful illustrations by Jack Seymour, but also Ruth Roff and other members of her team – Joanna Davey, Natalie Chen and Isobel Gillan – without whom this book would have stayed as an interesting idea rather than become the beautiful book you are holding.